Keep Off The Grass!

by
Walter Gilmour

with additional research by
Rhona Wilson

Nelson Monument, Glasgow Green.

First Published in the United Kingdom, 1996
By Richard Stenlake Publishing, Ochiltree Sawmill,
The Lade, Ochiltree, Ayrshire KA18 2NX
Telephone/fax: 01290 423114

ISBN 1 872074 25 1

Walter Gilmour

A Dundonian by birth, Walter Gilmour started his training in Horticulture as Dundee Parks Department's first apprentice. After spending some time with the Scottish Research Institute in Invergowrie, he went on to take his Diploma in Horticulture at the Royal Botanic Garden, Edinburgh.

On completion in 1959 he returned to Dundee as Senior Lecturer/Tutor in Horticulture. He held this post for several years before taking up an appointment with Livingston Development Corporation, in charge of Landscape Division at the start of the New Town.

For the following twenty-five years Walter held the post of Principal Horticultural Services Officer with the City of Glasgow Parks & Recreation Department, spearheading many of the City's' major projects.

During 1986 he was seconded to the Scottish Development Agency to act as Horticultural Advisor and Awards Co-ordinator prior to and during the Glasgow Garden Festival in the late 1980s.

On his return to the Department he represented the City at the thirteenth World Orchid Conference in New Zealand.

In 1990 he took early retirement and started as a Horticultural and Environmental Consultant. He now finds himself busier than ever.

Over the years Walter has been known in broadcasting circles, having presented a slot on Radio Clyde for seventeen years and guested with the Gardener's Question Time team on their Scottish visits, and more recently Classic Gardening Forum.

Since 1988 he has been involved off and on as a presenter with BBC's Scottish gardening programme Beechgrove Garden and now appears regularly each week as the other half of the "Hit Squad".

Dedication

Of the many Directorships of Glasgow's parks James Whitton and Sidney Arthur John Oldham stand out clearly and have both been a terrific inspiration to me. Whitton was in charge from the early 1890s when there were only a handful of parks, and achieved a great deal during his thirty year stretch when the department was developing at a rate of knots. My own boss, Arthur Oldham, was given the Directorship in 1964 but took his job far beyond its remit. Remembered as the man who got rid of the 'Keep Off the Grass' signs, Arthur believed that parks were there to be used and enjoyed by everyone freely. His tremendous enthusiasm and passion for the parks rubbed off on his employees and I'm proud to say that my old boss is also still a dear friend.

Acknowledgements

I'd like to thank Alison, my wife, for typing out my terrible hand-writing and also Ian Gordon of the Glasgow Room, Douglas Nesbit, Jean Marshall, Jack MacCallum, Rhona Wilson and Derek E. Black for their help with this book.

FOREWORD

Ironically, Glasgow began to acquire its numerous parks as a side-effect of the Industrial Revolution, when the city fathers started to establish them as an antidote to the polluted air of the city. The ancient grazing land of Glasgow Green was joined by the likes of Kelvingrove, Queen's and Alexandra Park, each acting as a 'lung' offering an opportunity for fresh air and exercise. Glasgow also used its parks to compete with other cities, staging lavish community events such as the International Exhibitions at Kelvingrove and Bellahouston. The parks have a historical legacy ranging from the domestic to the national. The Green was used by Bonnie Prince Charlie and his unpopular troops in 1746, while Queen's Park was the site of Mary Queen of Scots' disastrous Battle of Langside some two centuries earlier.

It's probably the humbler users of the parks such as you and I, however, who have the fondest memories of them. They are where we played, courted, strolled and watched the cycle repeat itself in our old age. These days the parks are vastly different from the formal gardens of the past. World War II saw the removal of the iron railings surrounding most of them and, together with the increasing popularity of cinema and television, the end of their special status. Although vandalism has been a problem, there have been some advantages from the loss of the authoritarian parkie. Park users no longer have to 'Keep Off the Grass!', and you'd be just as likely to hear techno music at a bandstand or visit a ski-slope as enjoy a recital or a nice game of bowls.

The parks came about as a result of a changing city and have had to continually adapt and deal with adversity – from decreasing funding to road developments. Glasgow has many parks, and this collection of pictures is not comprehensive, illustrating some but not all of the city's most popular playgrounds. At present Glasgow has more parks and open spaces per head of population than any city in Europe. That's a fantastic legacy and one that should be preserved for future generations.

Walter Gilmour, October 1996.

A shot on the boats at Alexandra Pond cost tuppence and was very popular with children during the summer months. Other facilities in the park at this time included a paddling pool and a Blind People's Hut. 60,000 people used the pool one summer according to a park report of 1878 – although no doubt there were a few regular paddlers counted in the total! The hut was apparently used to provide facilities for indoor sports, although it is difficult to imagine which ones would have been appropriate. The pond is now reserved strictly for the birds.

Children's Day in Alexandra Park, 1900. Not many children today would think it much fun to dance round a maypole, but this group look happy enough. Although most of the participants are girls, some boys have gathered round, eager to spy a girlfriend, classmate or sister.

The *Gardener's Chronicle* of 12 April 1884 reported that on one of the census days when numbers of people visiting the park were recorded, an incredible 20,000 people passed through Alexandra Park's gates. Saturday bands during the four summer months attracted an average of 30,000 spectators!

Despite being conveniently located near Townhead and Dennistoun, the site of Alexandra Park wasn't easy to cultivate. Not only was the area windswept and cold, but pollution from nearby industry made matters even worse. However, the establishment of trees was more successful than had at first been anticipated by parks staff, and today Alexandra is a well established and much loved leafy environment. No doubt the closure of Blochairn Works improved matters. Here, the gas works are visible at the north end of the park (it must have been one of Glasgow's clear days!)

The model yacht pond (photographed c.1900) was a popular venue for inter-city yacht club races and competitions, which were encouraged by the district works and tobacco factory workers. Many of the model yachts were lovingly made by their owners and were decorated with the elaborate fretwork popular at the time.

The entrance to Alexandra Park off Alexandra Parade, 1902. In 1866 the City Improvement Trust bought part of the estate of Haghill from its owner, William Stewart, for use as a park. This area was known as Wester Kennyhill. The park lands were expanded when Mr Alexander Dennistoun, owner of Easter Kennyhill, recognised that the proximity of a public park would make the development of his property more attractive. With this in mind, he donated a further five acres and the park was opened to the public in 1870 by the Prince and Princess of Wales.

Golf was played on Glasgow Green at least as early as the mid-eighteenth century, and the royal and ancient game was soon taken up in Alexandra Park too. Here, Bailie Steel tees off in the 1903 Municipal Golf Trophy competition. The trophy, which is still played for today, was unique in that it featured silver clubs with silver balls, with one of each added each year and inscribed to the winner. However, as it became progressively heavier, an inscribed plate was used instead. Many prominent Scottish golfers had their first lesson and developed a love of the game in Alexandra Park. In 1910 its eighteen hole course, which was laid out at Blackhill to the north-east of the park, charged the modest sum of thruppence a round. The site of the park's former bandstand was eventually converted into a driving range for golfers.

Some of the Ardgoil Estate forestry staff and their families outside the cottage at Ardkinglas, 1908. The heavily bearded gentleman was supposedly the oldest man in Glasgow! Ardgoil was gifted to the Corporation of Glasgow by Mr A. Cameron Corbett MP in 1908; previously he had gifted Rouken Glen to the city. Situated at the junction of Loch Goil and Loch Long, the estate, forty miles from the city, was incorporated into an afforestation scheme designed to tackle some of the social problems of the time. This provided work both for existing estate staff and the unemployed, as well as creating a source of revenue for the future. For many years Glasgow's George Square Christmas tree, along with those of many churches and public buildings, came from the Ardgoil estate.

Families en route to Ardgoil, June 1913. For a fortnight each summer, the Corporation arranged a daily steamer trip to the estate. These steamers took mothers and children from more congested parts of the city, who would not normally be able to afford a holiday, on the free day trip.

Drivers – most likely corporation transport staff – and helpers on one of the seasonal trips to Ardgoil. Glasgow families used the estate for a variety of recreational activities, such as Sunday School treats, picnics and holiday camps. Don't you just love the bow ties!

The annual picnic at Ardgoil, July 1913. For the children who attended them, these picnics were often their first experience of the countryside.

The piece of land that originally formed Bellahouston Park was acquired in 1895, with the addition of part of the lands of Dumbreck in 1901 and Ibroxhill in 1903. The latter purchase was made to provide a better entrance to the park, whilst preserving the well wooded grounds, shown here in the year they were acquired. Bellahouston's old mansion house was used as the family residence of the Parks' Director James Whitton until his death in 1925. It was later turned into a tearoom, which didn't do very well because of nearby rivals and was eventually demolished due to extensive dry rot.

Visitors entering the west gate of Bellahouston Park, off Dumbreck Road, in 1908. The shady walks and quiet retreats must have been particularly inviting, with the city chimneys belching great columns of sulphurous smoke not far distant. Mining for coal from the late eighteenth to the mid-nineteenth centuries left many areas of Glasgow susceptible to subsidence, and the park gatehouse, pictured here, was removed in the 1970s because of unstable foundations.

The view from the hill which forms the central feature of Bellahouston Park is still magnificent, although in contrast to today this 1912 photograph shows a Govan skyline cluttered with busy cranes. Work was long and hard at the shipyards and Bellahouston was the venue for all sorts of recreation – football, hockey, cricket, golf and bowling – and these activities were only temporarily suspended when the magnificent 1938 Empire Exhibition was held in the park.

Bellahouston's bandstand was eventually replaced by a more modern version. Today this has also disappeared, with a dry ski slope taking its place – a testimony to changing fashions. Ornate ironwork was popular for bandstands but not so popular with the departmental painters who had to maintain them.

The biggest event to take place in Bellahouston was the ambitious 1938 Empire Exhibition, located in the park because of its size and relative absence of formal walkways, a feature which allowed the designers complete freedom. As well as its status as the Second City of the Empire, 1938 was the fiftieth anniversary of Glasgow's first International Exhibition in Kelvingrove Park. With its suffering coal and shipping industries, the city was badly in need of the boost an exhibition could bring, and as such, the Empire Exhibition was conceived as a form of practical and spiritual support; promoting industry and raising morale. However, despite its positive intentions the exhibition was overshadowed by the looming Second World War, evidenced by the presence of the Services and Peace Pavilions.

The long, narrow pond to the right of this picture separated the buildings holding exhibitions from the 'Empire's Dominions and Colonies' area. Four very popular Canadian Mounties were usually stationed outside the Canadian Pavilion, whereas inside visitors could view a selection of stuffed native animals, amongst other exhibits – a rather sad way of celebrating a nation's vibrant wildlife! Other spectacles included a huge copper map and an outdoor mural illustrating Canadian life. Out of keeping with the rest of the exhibition buildings, the African Pavilion was built in the Dutch colonial style, although this didn't affect its popularity.

British Railways was one of five major firms which had their own pavilion outwith the main exhibition halls of the Palaces of Industry and Engineering. Covering five acres, the Palace of Engineering was the largest building on site and ominously decorated with murals of aeroplanes and warships. Inside visitors could view demonstrations of industrial processes and see various exhibits such as models of bridges and dams, and a huge revolving globe of the world. British Rail's building must have been a trainspotter's heaven, containing scale models of main routes and selling train tickets to any UK destination.

The Atlantic Restaurant was not only the exhibition's most exclusive eatery, but the focus of its opening ceremony. Its ship design was built around a granite monument which was unveiled by King George VI and Queen Elizabeth, and still stands today. Afterwards, the royals ate at the restaurant and possibly used the Royal Reception Rooms next to the Palace of Art. Their visit also included a trip up the striking Tower of Empire and a visit to the reconstructed Highland village.

The rather grandly named Tower of Empire quickly became known as the Tait Tower, after the exhibition's architect-in-chief, Thomas Smith Tait. He designed the observation tower to capitalise on the vantage point provided by Bellahouston Hill, most of which had to be left untouched to preserve its mature trees. This meant that there was very little room for the tower's foundations and a huge concrete block, still inside the hill today, had to be used to secure it. Tait wanted to break with previous exhibition styles, and judging by the functional, elegant lines of his buildings he certainly succeeded. In fact, 'modernist' was one of the criticisms lodged against the exhibition by those who preferred the old-fashioned African Pavilion. Tait, however, defended himself by stating that the designs were dictated by the use of certain materials. Uniformity across the exhibition was achieved by the control of colours, materials and design of secondary items such as bins and kiosks.

The east side of the park was taken over by Butlin's Amusement Park for the duration of the exhibition, and was considered to be separate from the main attractions. The amusement park was outside Tait's architectural control, although there were other exhibits within its confines including the Highland Clachan and the Indian Theatre. The latter charged a separate fee for entry and was built after the success of a similar attraction at the Second International Exhibition in 1911. One author tells the story of Queen Mary's unannounced visit to Butlin's. Ride operators were apparently besieged by hoards of people trying to get off moving amusements in order to get a look at the royal visitor!

Touted as being the same size as a small town, the Empire Exhibition took only fourteen months to build. Admission cost one shilling, the same price as Glasgow's first international exhibition fifty years earlier, and perhaps this liberality led to the event's financial downfall. Despite being its most successful crowd-pullers, the Highland Clachan, Tait Tower and ambitious Victoria Falls reconstruction weren't popular enough. With a mammoth attendance record of 12.5 million, the exhibition managed to make a loss that at around £130,000 was just as spectacular. I wonder what astronomical attendance would have been necessary to get it into profit! Various factors were blamed from the dismal summer weather to the impending war. A plan to reopen the site the following year was scrapped and, as with previous exhibitions, the site cleared. Today, all that remains in the park is the Palace of Art and the stone Peace Cairn which can be seen from Bellahouston's Rock Garden.

Glasgow's original botanic gardens were owned by the Royal Botanical Institute of Glasgow and supplied the Old College with specimens of medical plants. The gardens were moved around throughout the years – a tablet still exists marking a previous home at Fitzroy Place, Sauchiehall Street – and eventually arrived at the Great Western Road site in the 1840s. Ironically, it was the cost of this final move that resulted in the botanics slipping out of the institute's hands. Although the gardens were private and charged an entry fee, the cost of maintenance became overwhelming in the light of the financial outlay it took to get them to their prestigious West End site. Glasgow City took them over in 1891 on the condition that their research use would continue and the gardens supply Glasgow University to this day. Glasgow park railings such as these seen here had their spikes removed because of an accident in Queen's Park when a woman was horrifically impaled.

The ornamental lawns in the Botanic Gardens, Kelvinside, at the turn of the century. A member of staff standing at the rhododendron stares out a lad trying to ignore the 'Please Keep off the Grass' signs. The range of hothouses in the background were made of teak, which is highly durable and stands up well to high temperatures and heavy humidity. There are eleven displays inside the hothouses, devoted to some tremendous groups of plants including tropical ferns, orchids and begonias. Other educational displays include a grouping of 'economic plants' which can be used to produce commodities such as medicines, rubber, and sugar, and a chronological border designed to show when certain plants were introduced to Britain.

The Kibble Palace, with an area of 23,000 square feet, originally stood by the shores of Loch Long and was moved to its present spot in 1873 by owner John Kibble, who used it as a concert hall. (Incidentally, he approached Queen's Park with the idea first of all, but his offer was declined). Meetings of various sorts were regularly held there, including the rectorial addresses delivered to Glasgow University students by Gladstone and Disraeli, before the Botanics acquired full ownership and turned it into a conservatory in 1881. Today, a fine collection of tree ferns from Australia and New Zealand dominates its central dome.

Cambuslang's park was acquired around 1913, and for the most part has been left in its natural state, with many pleasant walkways. The one alongside the Borgie will be well remembered by courting lads and lasses from days gone by. In the middle of the eighteenth century the park was the site of religious fervour, set off by the local minister, at what is now called the Preaching Braes. Rev. William MacCulloch was known as the Ale Minister when he first arrived in the village because his boring sermons invariably sent all the men off to the pub. However, when he began preaching about the conversions of a populist preacher, George Whitefield, he started a religious revival of his own. In 1742, when the village population was a mere 1,000 strong, an estimated 30,000 pilgrims visited Cambuslang to hear McCulloch speak alongside popular preachers of the day.

The Cathkin Braes, known as the Guttie Park, originally formed a small part of the Cathkin estate. This was purchased in 1886 by a Mr James Dick, who gifted it to the city to celebrate his marriage the same year and subsequently sold the remaining land for building purposes. Mr Dick was a millionaire, owning a factory that produced boots and belting for heavy industry. The park's local nickname is apparently derived from the 'guttie' shoes that the factory produced. R.& J. Dick Ltd were well known throughout the Empire and had agents in the principal cities of the British Colonies and Dominions. Certain conditions were attached to Mr Dick's gifting of the Braes, and amongst other things he stipulated that the area should be held in perpetuity as a place of resort for the inhabitants of the City of Glasgow. The highest point in Cathkin Braes Park is called Queen Mary's Seat, the vantage point from which the queen supposedly witnessed the overthrow of her hopes at the Battle of Langside on 13 May 1568.

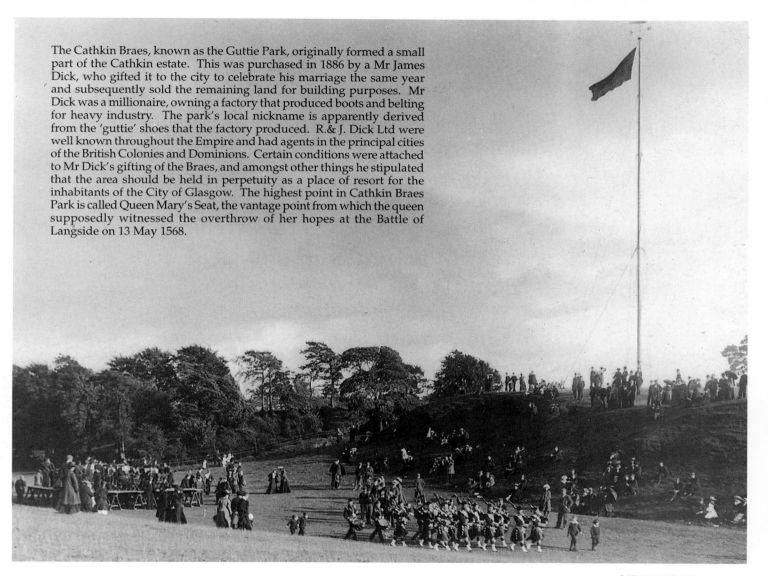

Dawsholm Park, situated north of the Forth and Clyde Canal at Temple, had origins in an offer by Sir Archibald Campbell, Bart of Succoth, to give the free lease of forty-three acres of woodland, known as the Belvidere Plantation, from his Garscube Estate. This area of the park was later purchased outright, and Sir Archibald included the site of shale bings in the sale – in view of the cost which would be entailed in levelling them to form a recreation ground. The levelling work in these 1920s photographs would have been carried out by the unemployed for the most part, as was the case with many parks works of the period. Dawsholm Park was formally opened in 1922.

Children on an outing from a city hospital enjoy a picnic in Elder Park, 1910. The boy on the left looks as if he's got an eye on his neighbour's cake!

Many families living in the poorer parts of Glasgow were seldom if ever able to get access to the countryside, but the Parks Committee in their wisdom brought nature to the city. A section of the 1901 International Exhibition at Kelvingrove was devoted to farm animals, with incubators set up so that children could watch chicks hatch from their eggs. Elder Park, with its deer enclosure and solitary llama, was a more permanent facility for Govan families at the turn of the century. There were also deer at Tollcross Park, reputedly shipped in from Japan.

Elder Park was purchased and presented to the Burgh of Govan in 1885 by the widow of John Elder, marine engineer and founder of Fairfield's Shipyard. This statue was erected to her memory in 1905 by public subscription. Glasgow acquired the park seven years later when Govan became part of the city through the Extension of Boundaries Act. When Mrs Elder presented her park to the burgh she stipulated that it was to be used for 'healthful recreation', and expressly forbade that games be played there at any time. The byelaws laid down were similar to those in force in Springburn Park in the north-east of the city, and seem incredibly arcane today. Amongst other restrictions, they stipulated that:

NO PERSON SHALL EXERCISE, OR BREAK IN A HORSE, ASS OR MULE.

NO CATTLE, SHEEP, PIGS OR GOATS ARE ALLOWED TO PASS THROUGH THE PARK.

NO PERSON SHALL WASH ANY CLOTHES IN THE LAKE IN THE PARK, NOR PLACE OR DRY CLOTHES IN THE PARK, OR ON THE RAILINGS.

NO PERSON SHALL BEAT, SHAKE OR CLEAN CARPETS, MATS OR RUGS IN THE PARK.

NO PERSON SHALL WADE, BATHE OR FISH IN THE LAKE. (What happened if your boat got stuck?)

NO PERSON SHALL DISCHARGE ANY FIREARM, OR SET OFF ANY BALLOON OR FIRE BALLOON.

NO PERSON SHALL SING, READ OR RECITE ANY PROFANE OR OBSCENE BALLAD. (Who would dare!)

NO PERSON SHALL EXPOSE WOUNDS OR DEFORMITIES INDUCING THE GIVING OF ALMS. (Mr Rab C. Nesbit please note).

Children pose for the camera by Elder Park pond, 1890. This was particularly popular with retired shipyard workers who built and sailed model yachts, passing their skills on to younger generations. These children would have been on their best behaviour and in awe of the resident parkie. However, the role of these uniformed authoritarians decreased with the advent of World War II. Most park railings were taken away as part of the war effort, and parks ceased to be so easy to patrol. Previously, parkies went around with a bell half an hour before closing to make sure the park was cleared. After this it was of course easy to stay on in the park unsupervised with some facilities suffering as a result.

A newly landscaped part of the thirty-five acre park in 1910. Profits from the Fairfield shipyard indirectly financed Elder Park, and a drinking fountain to the memory of company employees who died when HM Submarine K13 sank in trials off Gareloch in 1917 stands near the main gate. The offices of another shipbuilding company (Stephens) were once located within Elder Park. They occupied part of the former Linthouse Mansion, which stood near the river. The porch is all that remains of the mansion today.

For most of the nineteenth century, boating and regattas were the great spectator sport on the Clyde. Throughout the summer months regattas were held every Saturday, and attracted thousands along the length of the river between Nelson's Monument (on the right hand side of the photograph) and Rutherglen Bridge. In some respects it's astonishing that Glasgow Green still exists. Mr Clelland, the city's Statistician and Superintendent of Works, commissioned extensive borings in the park in the early 1820s, and concluded that an estimated half a million tons of coal lay below it. The city fathers couldn't resist the opportunity to capitalise on this find, and it was suggested that coal be mined to raise revenue, which could finance parks in the more affluent West End and southern parts of the city. There would have been subsidence of around one foot for every two feet mined, but the authorities reassuringly asserted that plenty of rubbish could be found to fill the gap! Not surprisingly, there was an outcry from East Enders outraged that their park was to be devastated for the benefit of richer areas. There was such a strong protest that, despite the temptations, the plan was dropped although it was mooted again in 1869 and 1888.

Children enjoying a paddle in the late 1920s in what was called the Sannie Pon'; no Mediterranean seas for this generation! There was a sandpit and paddling pool at Glasgow Green from 1914 onwards, both which were very popular, particularly during the Glasgow Fair when most holidays were spent at home. Unfortunately, the sandpits also proved irresistible to dogs and were removed in the interests of hygiene in the 1960s when safety (and liability) became more important issues.

Victorian carpet bedding was mainly fashionable in Glasgow's West End, although this photograph was taken in the flower garden at Glasgow Green. A time-served craft gardener (who would have undergone a four or five year apprenticeship) is pictured trimming the semi-tropical and half-hardy carpeted plants used for his star design, c.1912. In the 1901 Glasgow census around five hundred people listed themselves as gardeners, although this classification has changed in recent years. Time-served employees are now termed 'Craft Gardeners' whereas the former park labourers now get to call themselves Gardeners. Symmetry was the key with these complex bedding patterns, and although the colours of the designs were sometimes garish, the overall patterns were very effective. The plants used tended to be of a dwarf nature, providing two dimensional designs with colour from their foliage rather than flowers.

The grand Adam Arch still survives, although the authorities have never seemed certain about what to do with it. It once formed part of the Athenaeum or old Assembly Buildings which were built in Ingram Street in the early 1790s. However, Mr McLennan, who was appointed as Bailie to the Town Council in 1844 had the arch moved and re-erected at the north entrance of Glasgow Green in 1894. It was subsequently moved to Greendyke Street because of carriageway improvements. The poor old arch was later relocated a third time to its present resting place, where it forms a grand entrance and focal point for the green at its west end, opposite the High Court.

Apart from the People's Palace, the Humane Society House is the only other permanent building to have been built on Glasgow Green. Founded in 1790 to co-ordinate rescue efforts on the river, the society was run first of all by the Geddes family for several generations before being handed over to the Parsonages. Its officers were kept busy for a number of reasons. Asides from suicides and the occasional accidental death of a drunk, dares to go into the Clyde at low tide were common. What wasn't so commonly known was that the base of the river was made up of a very fine silt all too easy to get trapped in. Just as well, then, that Ben Parsonage was so knowledgeable of the Clyde's eddies and currents that he could estimate where a body would come out if he knew where it went in! The building seen here was eventually knocked down and replaced by a new one at the swing bridge.

It is incredible to think of the many safety measures incorporated into children's play areas today, compared with the basic facilities in this picture, taken around 1901. The open air gymnasium at the end of Caledonia Road was built in 1860 near the Humane Society house, and proved popular for many events including boxing, which before the introduction of the Marquis of Queensbury Rules in 1867 was often bare-fisted. You were considered a right Jessie if you couldn't reach the top frame and perform acrobatics! In recent years the gymnasium was immortalised by a mention in the Glasgow novel No Mean City.

Until the early years of the twentieth century, football on Glasgow Green was second only to the regatta as a major spectator sport. In fact, it could be said that the Green was the birthplace of Scottish football. Both Rangers (1873) and Celtic (1888) had their origins there. In the days before the First World War teams of supporters would march in procession behind a horse drawn brake displaying the team colours and banner. The eventual match result would be displayed in large letters on the side of the brake. Of course if the team lost the supporters were inclined to rally round to obscure the poor result. A Vale of Clyde brake club banner dating from 1900 is held at the People's Palace Museum and is brought out periodically for displays.

A quiet Sunday afternoon walk along the broad walks of Glasgow Green with strollers togged out in their Sunday best, 1910. This area of the park was known as Skinner's Green, on account of the flesh market which used to be held there. Public hangings also took place on the Green up until 1865. In the first half of the nineteenth century over seventy people were hanged for crimes ranging from robbery to high treason. The last was Dr Prichard who committed a double whammy by poisoning both his mother-in-law and his wife. The People's Palace Winter Gardens – a magnificent feat of structural engineering by James Boyd and Sons of Paisley – was added to the completed museum building in 1898.

The Winter Gardens' design is said to be based on the inverted hull of Nelson's flagship *Victory* and was probably chosen because of the building's proximity to the Nelson monument. The rounded lines, in keeping with other conservatories, would also have been necessary to shed wind and minimise damage to the potentially fragile glass building. Nevertheless, damage was done. The building began to deteriorate from the time of the two world wars when there was little available cash to spend on maintenance. This led to huge structural problems which resulted in the gardens being closed to the public. They were only saved, in fact, when it was discovered they would cost more to demolish than repair. The interior was re-landscaped and the Winter Gardens re-opened in 1978, on the exact day of their eightieth anniversary.

John Wright's Chairoplanes, photographed in the 1950s. Mechanised amusements such as these eventually replaced the Glasgow Fair, which was originally held on the Green but now signifies a holiday more than an event. It was the darker side of the fairs held at Jail Square which eventually led to their official banishment to Vinegarhill (along with the equally distasteful public hangings) in 1870. Fairs were adored by the common people and loathed by the clergy, who considered them an abomination. Certainly some of the side-shows sound unsavoury. Seedy Penny Theatres earned their keep by trading in 'filthy jokes' and people in the last stages of consumption were displayed for a price as macabre Living Skeletons. Survivors of this entertainment-genre existed at the Barras for many decades afterwards although fairground rides are now the sanitised norm at such events.

Green's Cinematograph, photographed in 1906. Outfits like this were probably a progression from the temporary wooden theatres which used to crowd Glasgow Green, providing entertainment for the working classes. From the 1840s there were a variety of disputes between these upstart theatres, which produced cheap, irreverent drama such as twenty minute Hamlets, and the licensed theatres with their official monopolies. The size of the temporary operations, which could sometimes seat over a thousand people, seem to have been threat enough, asides from the fact that they produced popular skits for a pittance. Although a petition with 60,000 signatures was raised in 1845 to get the theatres removed from the Green the end result was that the 'proper' establishments lost their right to run a cartel.

Templeton's ornate carpet works are a testimony to the feeling that both Glaswegians and their civic representatives have for the Green. In the late 1880s, when James Templeton approached the city fathers with plans for building a factory on its edge, he was told in no uncertain terms that any such building would have to enhance the area. To today's eyes he seems to have gone wonderfully over the top. His architect, Leiper, chose Venice's exotic Doge's Palace as a model, a rather whimsical subject for a flooring manufacturers. The factory was extended in 1957 to cover the area which was once the site of the wash house. After closing the building became a centre for small businesses, and today it is a magnet for tourists and the apprentice brick-layers who visit it as part of their training.

Gifted to the city by Lord Glenconner in 1914, this was never a large park, but provided a pleasant open space in a district that has seen a great deal of development in recent years.

The Gorbals burying ground in Rutherglen Road was acquired in 1885 and redeveloped in the early 1950s as a rest garden. Many poor families actually used the parks as a 'make-do' burial ground for infant deaths in the distant past – a testimony both to the poverty of the times and the infant mortality rate. Set against the walls of the Gorbals grounds are several interesting eighteenth century tombstones revealing the trades of the people buried there. Prior to the advent of the mower, motor scythe and strimmer, the scythe was the ultimate grass-cutting tool. Although particularly well suited for very long grass, these men were so skilful that they could shave a bowling green to almost 3/16" and not leave a mark on it. The scythe blades would be stone sharpened once an hour or so, a skill jealously guarded by the scythesmen. This picture was taken in 1900.

Govanhill Park was acquired by the Corporation in 1894. The area it occupied is almost square and was originally divided into two parts separated by a fence. One half was covered with ashes acquired from a nearby gas works, and allocated to boys aged twelve and under for playing football and other games. The remaining part was grassed over for use as a general play area. A small outdoor gymnasium (an equivalent to today's swing park) was provided in the grassy area. Many of the pieces of equipment in the swing park would seem quite dangerous in comparison to today's modern standards. This part of the park was apparently overseen by an elderly attendant and it would be no bad thing if someone, elderly or otherwise, would keep stray dogs in order in the park today.

Despite its small area, Govanhill Park has always been an asset to the community in this densely populated district, and was particularly popular in the earlier years of this century as this picture illustrates. However, what was once a leafy relief from the surrounding mass of tenements was sadly neglected. For many years the bandstand, which was added in 1903, stood lonely and covered with graffiti, and many of the elm trees originally planted in the park were removed after being affected by the Dutch Elm epidemic. In 1996 the park was upgraded to modern day standards and has now found a new role in the surrounding community.

These Govanhill 'tanner baw' players of 1910 would have thought the park facility a luxury, having practised their early ball skills in streets with passing traffic. Jackets formed posts and the game often progressed for hours, watched by wee brothers and sisters, not yet into ball skills. Note the stiff collars worn by some of the players.

Hogganfield Loch and grounds were acquired by the Corporation between 1820 and 1932, with the initial purchase of the Ruchazie Lands. The loch was constructed using horses and 'tipping bucket' carts to transport materials (these were formerly used in the coal industry) and progress was consequently slow. The original layout included a peninsula, although a link was later removed from this to form an island. This is now a bird sanctuary and in different seasons one can see heron, several species of duck, geese and numerous other birds. Motor boat and rowing trips were the big time for many visitors, with fifty-three acres of loch to cover, linked to seventy acres of grounds.

A group of children strolling by the Kelvin in 1901. Kelvingrove Park played host to International Exhibitions in both 1888 and 1901. These were Glasgow's contribution to a trend of civic competitiveness began by London's Crystal Palace Exhibition in the 1850s. The concept originally stemmed from fairs, but the exhibitions were more respectable events expressing Victorian pride at industrialisation and progress, whilst satisfying the curiosity of the masses. Glasgow's first exhibition received almost six million visitors, with profits contributing to the city's new art galleries, built nearby. The second offered an opportunity to open the new galleries in style. This picture shows the 1901 exhibition's Industrial Hall during its construction. This fantastic Arabian palace of a building was designed by architects who had very few restrictions on them. The main consideration was that exhibition buildings would be able to keep rain out for six months!

Sunday school children sing and form a ring o' roses by Kelvingrove's iron bandstand, 1900. The following year the bandstand was surrounded by contributions to the exhibition including the Saracen Fountain and Royal Bungalow, whilst it played host to numerous concerts. It was later removed to make way for a new amphitheatre.

One featured building at both international exhibitions was Van Houten's tearoom. During the 1901 exhibition the cocoa kiosk was located near the Rockery Bandstand and – in the face of the Boer War – France's rather small exhibition. It offered a serviette, biscuit and Royal Worcester cup of cocoa at the grand reduced price of one penny – not bad even for 1901 prices. Tea Rooms were an important part of Glasgow culture at the time and provided staple refreshments throughout the exhibitions. There certainly weren't many alternatives on offer. In 1901 only one license was granted for the selling of alcohol!

Feeding pigeons at the duckpond in Kelvingrove Park during the 1920s. At the time, the curator of the park tried to restrict the feeding of birds and squirrels within the park owing to the damage being caused to plant materials. However, this proved an impossible task as the regulars, both human and feathered, had made an indelible mark on Kelvingrove. The ornamental pond was always a favourite place for adults and children, who still delight in watching and feeding the waterfowl. The little island in the pond is said to be laid out in the shape of the island of Cyprus.

The new Kelvingrove Amphitheatre attracted not only the best orchestras and bands from all over the world, but also thousands of spectators eager to pay admission in all weather. Outdoor music was very popular with Glasgow inhabitants and the park meetings were always well attended. Music also figured strongly in the two international exhibitions. One of the most stunning buildings at the 1901 event was the concert hall with its saucer dome. There were daily recitals and band music, although these were not quite up to the world class standards some would have demanded. Free music was a great crowd-puller, but charges were eventually instated allowing better concerts to be put on.

The Robert Stewart Memorial Fountain, made by James Sellars and James Mossman, was erected in Kelvingrove Park in 1872. During the 1901 exhibition it was flanked by a series of Irish cottages used to promote the country's weaving industry. Unlike exhibitions in venues such as Bellahouston Park, Kelvingrove already had a restricting layout of walkways and ornaments meaning the new buildings had to jostle for space with the permanent fixtures. The fountain was financed by the city water commission to commemorate Lord Provost Stewart, who eagerly pursued the project of bringing Loch Katrine water into the city. The figure at the top of the fountain is said to represent Sir Walter Scott's Ellen, the Lady of the Lake. After being vandalised, the fountain was restored in 1988, although there is no water in it.

Kelvingrove Park was acquired in 1852 and expanded thirty years later. There was strong opposition against the park in the beginning because, outrageously, there was no space for games and it was considered to be more akin to a garden. The art galleries were of course the permanent legacy of the two successful international exhibitions. Originally, Glasgow's main art collection was housed at the McLellan Galleries, named after the Bailie who donated his paintings to the city. However, this building was considered to be a fire risk and plans were made for a safer venue, a fortuitous move as the galleries were seriously damaged by fire in the mid-1980s. This picture shows the Kelvin Way bridge under construction. After being damaged during a bomb raid in the Second World War, some of its statues ended up in the Kelvin and the bridge wasn't restored until 1951.

Fountain and University, Kelvingrove, Glasgow.

1254

The neo-Gothic spires of Glasgow University, Gilmorehill. Originally, the university was located in the High Street. In its East End location labourers, industry magnates (such as the tobacco lords), and academics all lived and worked close together. From the 1850s, however, the middle classes began to move to the more spacious and leafy suburbs of the West End. Twenty years later the University relocated, confirming the social split. Its entrance on University Avenue was built with old-fashioned crow steps to echo the former Old College building.

A display from the 1922 Glasgow and West of Scotland Horticultural Society's International Flower Show. This event took place in the old Kelvin Hall, and the display is proudly fronted by Mr James Whitton, Director of Parks and Gardens, and his able staff. The exhibit occupied an area of 3,000 square feet and was comprised of exotic plant material brought to the show by horse and covered carts from the city's conservatories and stove houses. Mr Whitton, JP VMH, retired in the following year, having served the city as Director of Parks for over thirty years. When he took charge of the department's responsibilities Glasgow had five parks. By the time he retired, the city had thirty-one, plus numerous open spaces, and the department employed 1,250 staff.

With attractions including a nine hole golf course and two bowling greens, Knightswood Park has always been extremely popular. Purchased from the housing department in 1929 at a cost of £41,000, the choice of location was ideal, amidst what was one of the city's largest housing estates at the time.

The fabulous Tower de Paris Tearoom, complete with indoor palms, was situated at the Netherlee end of the park at what is now McLaren Place. Its sophisticated, almost nautical design makes it look like a refugee from one of the International Exhibitions. From the looks of the fancy boxes piled behind the counter it sold a variety of chocolate delicacies in a addition to a humble cuppa. The park's original tearoom was in the mansion house, which was being used as a Nature and Information Centre by the 1980s.

The Tower de Paris was built in the 1920s, just when tearoom culture was beginning to die out. Cafe society blossomed in Glasgow around the turn of the century when the city was prosperous (for manufacturers) and there were plenty of people with time and money to spare for eating out. Miss Cranston was probably the most famous proprietor, with her city establishments designed by local artists such as Charles Rennie Macintosh. Tearooms began to lose their popularity during the depressing time of the First World War, and never really recovered since they didn't adapt to changing tastes. However glamorous it looks, the Tower de Paris wouldn't have thought to compete with the tearooms of old – a visit to it would have just counted as part of a day out to the park.

Linn Park was originally part of Hagtonhill Estate, which belonged to the Maxwells of Pollok. The main avenue – leading to the River Cart – is lined with tall lime trees which are well over 130 years old. Within the park bounds the old Ha'penny Bridge, known as such in deference to larger Scottish bridges which cost a penny to cross, spans the river. After he read a letter complaining about the state of the bridge in the *Evening Times*, Arthur Oldham, Parks' Director at the time, immediately had it spruced up, much to the delight of park visitors. Linn Park was acquired in 1919. It was expanded by the addition of the lands of Cathcart Castle in 1927 and, six years later, by an area formerly known as Court Knowe. The shelter in this picture was used by Sunday Schools and community groups when Glasgow's weather ruined summer picnics.

Allotments were used as part of the Dig for Victory morale campaign during the Second World War, but have been around a lot longer than that. 'Allotment' originally referred to a plot of land awarded to a labourer to build a cottage on, but the term was eventually applied to a garden. In the 1840s a Select Committee on Allotments decided that more such facilities should be provided. As well as providing added food for poor families, it was hoped that the garden plots would improve the health of those who worked on them and keep them out of the beer shop, such were the social problems of the time. Victoria Gardens, Rutherglen, finally settled at the above site in 1912 after previous stints at Alleysbank and Claudesbush. The Residential Hospital now occupies the site of the gardens.

ENTRANCE TO OVERTOUN PARK, BURNSIDE.

80686.

This picture looks down Broomieknowe Road towards the entrance to Overtoun Park. The house on the right of the picture was built by Charles and Agnes Geddes in 1903 and was the first house in Rodger Drive, originally isolated and surrounded by fields. The New Victoria Garden Allotments appear to the left.

Originally known as The Chesters, the estate that made up Overtoun Park was bought by Lord Overtoun (proprietor of the town's chemical works) and gifted to Rutherglen in 1908. This philanthropic gesture didn't really compensate for the chemical waste left by the family business, which is still a massive problem today. Overtoun is the site of one of the few remaining Victorian bandstands in Glasgow parks. Gifted by James Fleming, it may also be the most well travelled, having been transported to the Stoke-on-Trent National Garden Festival in 1986 as Glasgow's token of friendship. Although Ruglonians were outraged at the time (the cheek of Glasgow taking our bandstand!) it was returned in 1989 none the worse for wear, after a stint at the Glasgow Garden Festival.

Phoenix Park recreation ground, 1911. The area occupied by the park was originally owned by the Phoenix Foundry, which produced cannon for use by the British Army before the Crimean War. Situated off Garscube Road, Phoenix owed its origins to the Glasgow's Health Committee which was involved in establishing small parks for deprived areas. It had excellent facilities for children including swings and separate gymnasia for each sex, and was a popular spot for whiling away a spare hour or two. The ornate fountain fronting the bandstand was gifted by 'Sweetie' Buchanan. Sweetie was one of the Buchanan brothers who owned the nearby confectionery works. One of the largest of its kind in the city, the works ran its machinery twenty-four hours a day. Sadly, Phoenix Park was obliterated by roadworks and development in the late 1950s.

69157 JV

Pollok Park was gifted to the city in 1967 by the Maxwell McDonald family, vastly increasing the acreage that had been open to the public as a park since 1911. The beautifully landscaped gardens within the park are of great horticultural value, and were created by the late Sir John Stirling Maxwell, who died in 1958. Shawmuir Lodge (above) was one of three lodges built as gateways to Pollok Estate, and now marks the main entrance to the country park. The other two have the family motto 'I am ready, gang forward' carved into the walls. Apparently Sir John's daughter was obsessed by horses, and uninterested in the estate's beautiful grounds, although she felt obliged to attend meetings of a local horticultural group. Members were treated to a speech from her on a rhododendron flower now famed for its brevity. 'This is a rhododendron. It's red, it doesn't have any smell and it grows at Pollock.'

As in many other parks, watching the band at weekends and on public holidays was a popular pastime for visitors to Queen's. This ornate iron bandstand was made in Glasgow, although it was later moved to Duchess Park in Motherwell, with the open-fronted building that replaced it still standing today. The group standing at the edge of this crowd would have had some difficulty in hearing, but going to see the bands wasn't just about listening to music. In a time when fraternising with the opposite sex was still strictly regulated, an outing to the park provided an opportunity to dress up in your finery and meet potential suitors in a chaperoned environment.

Queen's Park c.1906. In summer 1907 the park gates were altered to frame the entrance with art nouveau style stone pillars, although other more grandiose plans were never realised. Park designer Sir Joseph Paxton had originally intended to build winter gardens and a conservatory on the terrace beyond the granite staircase where they would overlook the city. Paxton was famous for his design of Hyde Park's Crystal Palace (1851), although there was no opportunity for spending that type of money in Glasgow, and the plans were rejected by John Carrick, city Master of Works, due to their extravagance.

Queen's Park's new glass corridor and propagation houses were built in 1905 on the hill opposite Battlefield Monument. These eventually replaced the old Camphill hothouses which were removed in the 1930s. Seasonal plant displays in the park were regularly promoted by handbills and adverts displayed on tramcars throughout the city. As strange as it may seem to today's sophisticated audiences, these were immensely popular and attracted queues of visitors at weekends. The chrysanthemum display in this picture would be the envy of any grower today.

The terrace where Sir Joseph Paxton's conservatory was to be built measures a massive 750 feet by 140 feet. When plans for a giant glasshouse were scrapped, the perfectly levelled site was used for a formal Dutch flower garden, which took over 40,000 seasonal bedding plants before being modified in 1930. One of Queen's Park's finest features is its views, and up from the terrace is a raised mound from which the Campsie Hills and Ben Lomond can be seen. This elevated position is also particularly good for the plants which thrive in the clean air.

A pleasant spring day in 1904. It is strange to imagine that when proposals to purchase Pathead farm (the site of Queen's Park) were made in 1857, one of the principal objections was that it was too far from the city to be useful to its inhabitants. In the end, only a casting vote by the Lord Provost carried its purchase, and time soon proved that the promoters of the scheme were wise in their choice. The park was opened to the public in the early 1860s, and many of the smaller burghs which used it were absorbed into Glasgow thirty years later as a result of the City Extension Act. Legend has it that bodies from the Battle of Langside are buried in the Deil's Kirkyard at the back of the park's pond, but excavations have so far drawn a blank.

Richmond Park was purchased for a set price per acre in 1898. During the process of transforming the land into a park, Rutherglen Road was widened and several old 'single end' buildings demolished. Due to overcrowding, these had been subject to epidemics such as typhus in the past. Jenny's Burn (also known as Mall's Myre Burn) was supposedly named after Jeanie Allan. Her father, the Glasgow textile merchant, had a magnificent residence on the north side of the Green and built a tunnel, known as Allan's Pen, for the public to walk through so he wouldn't be disturbed by the sight of riff-raff on his way down to the Clyde. Glasgow weavers were so outraged by his presumption that they refused to work for him. It was a good riddance indeed when a flood swept the offending pen away. At one time there was talk of developing a 'shop window' bulb display at Richmond along the lines of Holland's Keukenhof Gardens near The Hague but the plan never came to anything.

Rouken Glen's walled garden was enclosed on three sides, with railings to the front. The pathway the women are standing next to was its entrance. To the right, the steps led to the terrace, part of the mansion house. Large concrete containers would rarely be used in such an elevated position in public parks today, and wouldn't be planted with dangerously spiky Agave plants!

The parks department was rather precious about Rouken Glen when it opened in 1906. At first the public were only allowed to use it two days a week, and Rouken Glen Football Club received short shrift when it inquired about the possibility of playing in the grounds. Access was increased, however, and at one time there were few Glaswegians who hadn't fed the ducks or rowed a boat on Rouken Glen pond. In the depression years between the wars trips to the park were extremely popular for family outings and picnics. Transport was available by tram and train, and the bus service to Giffnock which was introduced later became the most popular option. Looking at this William Fullerton photograph its easy to imagine the cries of 'It's ma shot on the oars Maw – she's had her turn,' and 'Look, behave yersel or you'll be on the next tram hame tae Springburn.'

Rouken Glen, situated six miles from the city centre, has some wonderful stories attached to it. The lands, originally known as Birkenshaw, were presented by James V to Lord Eglinton in 1530 when his son Hugh Montgomery got married. The estate's name changed to Thornliebank on a whim of new owners, the Crums, when they redeveloped the mansion house in the 1860s. Many romantic tales of the park have accumulated, absorbed by time and enhanced by the natural beauty of the spot. According to history, William Wallace found shelter there, while the notorious nineteenth century murderess Madelaine Smith used the mansion as a summer residence. Lord Rowallan bought the park as a philanthropic gift for Glasgow in 1904, and its name was changed to Rouken Glen after the estate's old mill a couple of years later. The waterfall at the head of Rouken Glen is fed by the Auldhouse Burn, which rises in the Mearns district and forms a fine cascade as it rushes over the rocks in the park. After some debate, it was decided to introduce an informal boating pond into the park in 1924. This incorporated planted islands of rhododendron and native birch, and small bogeys were used to transport loads of red Giffnock sandstone into the area to form islands and shore the bankings.

Bandstand, Rouken Glen

69178

After the Second World War the standard of living in Britain rose, and television became the dominant form of entertainment. Visits to outdoor bandstands such as Rouken Glen's became less of a treat and, like many others, this one has been removed. In this picture the performers are surrounded by hordes of empty seats. Using one of these hinged, iron seats inside the ring cost a penny, and most of these music fans seem to have decided to stand.

THE STEPS TO THE WATERFALL, ROUKEN GLEN.
E 02895

OLD MILL IN ROUKEN GLEN.
57721. JV

There were two cotton mills in Rouken Glen's vicinity, but the park was named after the grain mill pictured above. Used by local farmers and known as Rockandmyll, its roots can be traced back to the twelfth century. However, the mill was demolished in 1879 as part of a modernisation programme carried out by the Crums. This included landscaping, tree planting and the infill of an old quarry, which the family originally earned a lot of their money from before demand for blond freestone declined.

The walk to the waterfall at the head of the glen, passing the ruins of the old mill en route, was very popular with visitors to Rouken Glen. The 'printer's stone', above the waterfall, was the place where apprentices of the Thornliebank Calico Print Works traditionally celebrated the end of their training, with the help of their first drop of the hard stuff!.

During World War I the Red Cross inspected Rouken Glen with the aim of using the mansion and grounds as a war hospital, a plan that proved too costly and was dropped in 1917. The park seemed destined for war-time use, however, since it was requisitioned by the War Office soon after the beginning of the next war. Not many changes were made by the army, asides from the addition of some military works built in the north-west corner along with a rifle-range. The park was returned to Glasgow in 1945 but seemed rather the worse for wear. By 1967 the dilapidated mansion house had to be demolished, and in 1984 Rouken Glen received a huge blow when Glasgow District decided that it was too much of a financial drain on its funds. Thankfully, Eastwood District took over its management and the park has since been rejuvenated with the addition of a garden centre, gatehouse gallery and boat house tea room.

Taking a break at the Rouken Glen Road entrance to the park. Having delivered his mail to the Mansion House in the park, this local postie would then walk to Eastwood and Giffnock – to think that some mail could be delivered on the same day it was posted!

Ruchill Park, acquired in 1892, gave tremendous views over Glasgow. To emphasise its choice location, Mr Whitton, Superintendent of Parks, arranged the dumping of 24,000 cart-loads of waste material from the building of Ruchill Hospital to form a flagpole-topped mound known locally as Ben Whitton. Apparently the owner of the ground at the south-east end of the park wanted to sell it off to the Corporation and built a tenement block on it when Glasgow declined the offer. Legend has it that this vengeful blocking of the mound's view was a prime reason for its artificial heightening. This 1898 picture looks down on the Forth and Clyde canal towards the newly formed paths and plantings, where 600 of Glasgow's unemployed men had tamed the bleak, uneven ground during the five previous years.

Ruchill Park originally belonged to Ruchill Estate before it became part of the old Burgh of Maryhill. Here, the 7th Scottish Rifles Pipe Band strikes up in front of the park's bandstand while members of the Glasgow Postal Band take a welcome break. The mound, also known as the Spion Kop, (after the famous Boer War battle on a hill of the same name) is on the far right of this picture, taken c.1912. Although the mound's four hundred foot height should ensure a good view, smog from Glasgow's industries often made it redundant. On a good day it is now possible to see several landmarks including the cathedral, Tinto hill and even Arran. The smoke may have disappeared, but sadly the tourists have yet to come flocking to Ruchill Park – even if it does offer a bird's eye view of the city.

Situated on Balgrayhill at over 300 feet above sea level, the site of Springburn Park has always been exposed and windswept, although it offers excellent views over the city and beyond. When the park was acquired, it was an indifferent piece of agricultural land with the remains of an ironstone pit in one corner and a disused quarry in another. It took three years to develop, with its designers making use of these original features and transforming the latter into a rockery. Two natural ponds were also modified and extended, providing a breeding place for ducks and waterfowl, but the principal attraction for children was the yacht and boating pond, which was particularly well patronised during the summer. In this picture the old Springburn water tower, situated at the top of the park's reservoir, looms in the background. Now demolished, the tower had sun-recording instruments and was used by the Edinburgh Meteorological Office for weather readings from 1896.

Springburn was originally a small, rural village before evolving into a sprawling manufacturing area. After land for the park was acquired in 1892, a programme of landscaping was quickly undertaken and completed. James Reid, of Hydepark Locomotives fame, gifted a magnificent bandstand plus £10,000 towards building materials for the Winter Gardens, which were completed in 1900. This picture shows the unveiling of the James Reid Monument. As a token of appreciation for the generous gifts made to the city by his family, the people of Springburn and district erected this life-size monument to James Reid after his death in 1894. His son Hugh, a senior partner in the firm Neilston Reid and Co. of Hydepark and director of the Clydesdale Bank, was later honoured by a memorial fountain in the park. Bowler and tile hats appear to have been the order of the day for the ceremony.

The winter garden provided an all year round focal point for Springburn Park, and delighted its visitors with exotic floral displays. The central structure was later extended by the addition of four wing houses. There were many fine Palms, Mimosa, Tree Ferns and other exotic plant genus inside, and its viewing gallery once displayed the finest floral displays in the country. Owing to vandalism and fire damage, the winter garden was closed in the mid 1980s, and currently lies in ruins.

Before 1909 the site of Balgray's neat recreation ground at Springvale Place was filled with two-storey slums. These were demolished and replaced with a main road and small park in 1911. The white tiled unicorn fountain was the focal point of the grounds and, along with the playground itself, the gift of Hugh Reid of the North British Locomotive Company. In the early 1980s the area lost the 'swings' when park and fountain were swept away to make room for a new road and sports centre. The unicorn fountain was fortunately saved and installed in Springburn Park. Part of Springburn North Church is visible to the left of the picture; the local ropeworks stood just to the right of this.

At the end of the nineteenth century the population of Glasgow's eastern districts was immense and growing fast. Great difficulty was had in securing a suitable site for a park to meet the needs of people living in the area, although the problem was eventually solved with the acquisition of Tollcross Estate in 1897. This unique property was long in the possession of James Dunlop, proprietor of the Clyde Ironworks, and his planting did much to improve the grounds. These were well wooded and included several genus of weeping trees, including a trio known the as 'three sisters', planted by the sisters of a former owner. A stream running through the grounds fed a small pond, which was well stocked with waterfowl, although after a drowning incident it was filled in. The International Rose Trial Garden, planted in recent years on the lawns west of the house, is a superb credit to the park's present day staff.

Tollcross Park was opened by Lord Provost Sir David Richmond on Queen Victoria's Diamond Jubilee. Bailie A.G. Macdonald , an ex-convenor of the Parks Committee, presented his glasshouses and collection of plants to the park, forming the nucleus of hot houses that were enjoyed by the people of Shettleston for many years. Plans for the Winter Gardens were being made in 1899 and Macdonald's gift gave them a much needed boost. Sadly, the plant houses were allowed to fall into ruin in later years, although funding from the National Lottery's Heritage Fund is now being used to give Tollcross a reprieve. The conservatories will be rebuilt and upgraded in keeping with the new swimming pool and leisure complex built recently in the east end of the park. The gravel ditches around the park's bowling green (above) were much hated on account of the damage they could do to bowls!

I don't know whether it's more striking that a woman is feeding deer in Glasgow city centre, or that the dirt track she is standing on is now the main road at Tollcross! Many parks or common greens in Glasgow were historically used for grazing. In its time Glasgow Green was home to herds of cattle, while sheep were brought in to several parks as an economic and labour-saving means of keeping the grass trim. But the deer in this picture were introduced to give city dwellers a taste of nature rather than to work. The lawn eventually became Tollcross Park's International Rose Trial Garden, while the destiny of at least one of the deer that lived in the park is certain. The last one, Bobby, was preserved by a taxidermist and put on display at Tollcross Museum. He was later removed to a store at Kelvingrove Galleries, but is still exhibited periodically.

To people from Tollcross and Parkhead, the Cock Robin exhibit, once on display in the Children's Museum, is legendary. First put on show in 1906, the exhibit shows the ill-fated robin and his sparra' assassin represented by equally unlucky stuffed birds. It was on display in the museum until it closed in 1976. After the museum closed Cock Robin became part of a travelling exhibit run by the Open/Glasgow Museum through which it visits the libraries or smaller museums that request it. Having became rather battered, the Cock Robin display was restored in 1990.

The grounds of Victoria Park were originally feued from their owner Gordon Oswald in 1886.

Perhaps if they'd been used for some other purpose the fantastic Fossil Grove would never have been discovered. It was only when workmen were forming a park walkway through the bottom of the old Knowe Quarry in 1887 that they uncovered 350 million year old fossilised tree stumps. Work on the pathway immediately ceased and the fossils were protected by a glass roofed building, heated to prevent weathering damage. Previously, fossil stumps had been spotted at Balgray in 1825 and in Gilmorehill in 1868, but this was the first attempt at preserving them. Quite rightly, this corner has now become the most popular part of the park and attracts visitors from all over the world. The fossils are solid stone casts of the insides of several scale trees, so called because of the scaly pattern left when they shed their leaves. The strongest part of a scale tree was its bark, whilst the soft core rotted away quickly when the trees died and their trunks broke apart. The hollow stumps and roots then filled with water which washed in sand, later being consolidated to form sandstone. Hard though it may be to believe, Whiteinch was a flourishing rain forest 350 million years ago, and the organic matter that rotted down from the rest of the trees made up the reserves of coal that have been mined in the area in more recent years.

Extensions to Victoria Park in 1894 and 1909 allowed the development of some excellent new features including this magnificent bandstand, which attracted audiences of 107,500 during the 1913 season of twenty-three performances. Mr Whitton, Superintendent of Parks, noted that after the outbreak of the First World War in the following year, attendance figures dropped to 59,000 for the same number of performances. In recent years the park has contracted in size, with much of its east end replaced by an approach road for the Clyde Tunnel.

The bowling green shelter at Victoria Park, photographed c.1894, could hardly be considered palatial! With its ancient wooden guttering the green is also behind the times; the slope of grass down to it would be at the precise angle demanded by Bowling Green Association rules. Bowling was a sport that filtered down from merchants and the gentry to the ordinary working classes. In the eighteenth century the working day was so long and arduous that most men and women didn't have the time or energy for pastimes outwith conversation and the partaking of alcoholic beverage. Early versions of games such as bowls, golf and football were played, however, and part of their attraction was that natural surfaces could be used, avoiding the need for expensive purpose-built facilities. Proper bowling greens began to be laid out in the nineteenth century as clubs started to compete with each other, and the sport increased in popularity as the working week shortened and wages rose. In the fields beyond at Jordanhill a pair of horses turn the hay on what would appear to be a pleasant summer's day, judging by the young lady with her parasol.